Read-About® Geography

New Mexico

By Cynthia Walker

Consultant
Donna Loughran
Reading Consultant

Children's Press®
A Division of Scholastic Inc.
New York   Toronto   London   Auckland   Sydney
Mexico City   New Delhi   Hong Kong
Danbury, Connecticut

Designer: Herman Adler Design
Photo Researcher: Caroline Anderson
The photo on the cover shows Angel Peak, Nacimiento Badlands.

Library of Congress Cataloging-in-Publication Data

Walker, Cynthia.
  New Mexico / by Cynthia Walker ; consultant, Donna Loughran.
    p. cm. — (Rookie read-about geography)
  Includes index.
  ISBN 0-516-22755-6 (lib. bdg.)   0-516-25933-4 (pbk.)
  1. New Mexico—Juvenile literature. 2. New Mexico—Geography—
Juvenile literature. I. Loughran, Donna. II. Title. III. Series.
  F796.3.W35 2004
  917.89—dc22
                                                    2004000472

Where can you find this cave?

Carlsbad Caverns

It is in New Mexico!

New Mexico is the
fifth largest state in
the United States.

It is in the southwestern
part of the United States.

CANADA

WASHINGTON
OREGON
IDAHO
MONTANA
NORTH DAKOTA
SOUTH DAKOTA
WYOMING
MINNESOTA
WISCONSIN
MICHIGAN
NEW HAMPSHIRE
VERMONT
MAINE
MASSACHUSETTS
NEW YORK
NEBRASKA
IOWA
NEVADA
UTAH
COLORADO
KANSAS
ILLINOIS
INDIANA
OHIO
PENNSYLVANIA
WEST VIRGINIA
RHODE ISLAND
CONNECTICUT
NEW JERSEY
DELAWARE
MARYLAND
CALIFORNIA
MISSOURI
KENTUCKY
VIRGINIA
Washington, D.C.
ARIZONA
NEW MEXICO
OKLAHOMA
ARKANSAS
TENNESSEE
NORTH CAROLINA
ALABAMA
GEORGIA
SOUTH CAROLINA
MISSISSIPPI
TEXAS
LOUISIANA
FLORIDA

North
West   East
South

ALASKA   CANADA
MEXICO
HAWAII

5

Many Mexican Americans live in New Mexico. So do many Native Americans.

Native American boy

The people and land make New Mexico special. They call New Mexico the "Land of Enchantment."

The state flag tells of
New Mexico's history.
The rays in the flag
stand for the sun.

This sun sign came
from Native Americans
called the Zia people.

The roadrunner is the state
bird of New Mexico.

Rattlesnakes and black widow spiders also live in New Mexico. So do black bears, coyotes, and mountain lions.

Black bear

The state flower is the yucca (YUCK-uh). The yucca grows in many places in New Mexico.

Cactus

Cactus and mesquite (mes-SKEET) trees grow in the desert.

Chama River Valley

There are many different kinds of land in New Mexico.

There are mountains, canyons (KAN-yuns), flat lands, and rocky deserts.

The Rio Grande flows
through the mountains.
It carries water south.
So does the Pecos River.

Farmers use water from
rivers for their crops
and animals.

Rio Grande

18

In the northwest, New Mexico has large hills with flat tops. These hills are called mesas (MAY-suhs).

Long ago, Native Americans built small cities on the mesas. These cities are called pueblos (PWEB-lohs).

New Mexico has three major cities. The city with the most people is Albuquerque.

Las Cruces (lahs KROO-ses) is in the middle of rich farmlands. Santa Fe is the state capital.

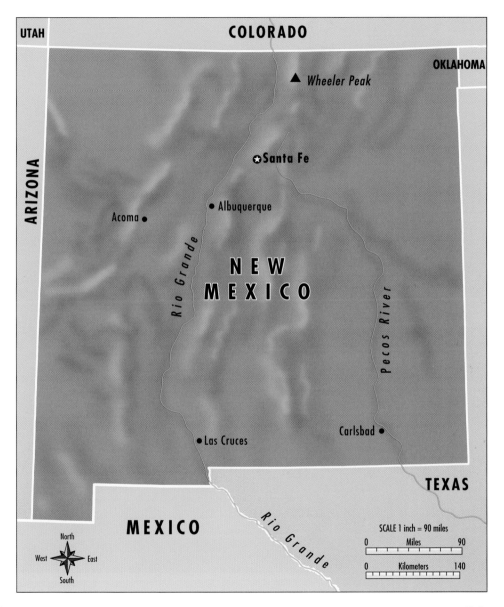

UTAH

COLORADO

OKLAHOMA

▲ *Wheeler Peak*

ARIZONA

✪Santa Fe

● Albuquerque

Acoma ●

Rio Grande

NEW
MEXICO

Pecos River

Carlsbad ●

● Las Cruces

TEXAS

MEXICO

Rio Grande

North
West ✦ East
South

SCALE 1 inch = 90 miles

| 0 | Miles | 90 |

| 0 | Kilometers | 140 |

21

Oil workers

People in New Mexico
do many kinds of jobs.

Some are scientists who
work in labs. Others work
for oil companies and
other places.

New Mexico has many
farms and ranches.

Ranchers raise cattle
and sheep.

Sheep ranch

Harvesting chili peppers

Farmers grow crops like
pecans and chili peppers.

New Mexico is famous for its chili peppers. People visit the Hatch Chili Festival. They watch the parade and eat spicy food.

Have you ever rode in
a hot air balloon?

You can do this and
many other things in
New Mexico.

Hot air balloons in Albuquerque

Words You Know

cactus

cave

chili peppers

flag

30

mesa

roadrunner

Rio Grande

yucca

31

Index

About the Author

Cynthia Walker is an author and illustrator of children's books. She lives in New York. Cynthia likes to vacation in the southwestern United States.

Photo Credits

Photographs © 2004: Bob Clemenz Photography: cover, 14; Buddy Mays/Travel Stock: 11, 12, 31 bottom right; Corbis Images: 18, 31 top left (Kevin Fleming), 27 (Catherine Karnow), 26, 30 bottom left (Danny Lehman), 22 (Charles E. Rotkin); Dave G. Houser/HouserStock, Inc.: 7 (Jan Butchofsky-Houser), 10, 31 top right (Ben R. Frakes), 13, 25, 29, 30 top left (Rankin Harvey), 17, 31 bottom left (Dave G. Houser), 9, 30 bottom right (Christie Parker); Stone/Getty Images/Chad Ehlers: 3, 30 top right; The Image Works/Dick Doughty/HAGA: 6
Maps by Bob Italiano.